What's in this book

This book belongs to

_____

艾文很忙！ Ivan is busy!

学习内容 Contents

沟通 Communication

说说闲暇活动
Talk about leisure activities

生词 New words

★	时间	time
★	功夫	kung fu
★	唱歌	to sing
★	跳舞	to dance
★	上网	to go online
★	运动	to do sports
★	再	again, once more
	照片	photo
	游泳	to swim
	舒服	well
	游戏	game
	生病	to get sick
	疼	to ache

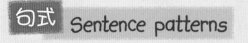

句式 Sentence patterns

我要运动，运动，再运动。
I will keep doing sports.

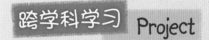

跨学科学习 Project

了解京剧，设计京剧脸谱
Learn about Beijing Opera and
design a facial make-up pattern

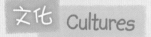

文化 Cultures

中国功夫
Chinese kung fu

Get ready

1 What do you do in your spare time?

2 What is your favourite leisure activity?

3 Ivan plays badminton and dances and sings with his friends during the holidays. Is he busy?

shí jiān
时间

武尚

gōng fu
功夫

放假了，艾文很忙，时间不够用。
星期一，他学中国功夫。

chàng gē
唱歌

zhào piàn
照片

tiào wǔ
跳舞

星期二，他学唱歌和跳舞。老师还
给他拍了照片。

星期三，他想叫伊森一起去游泳，
但是伊森不舒服。

伊森因为天天上网打游戏，所以生病了，头疼。

yùn dòng
运动

"你应该多运动，像我一样，就没时间生病了。"艾文说。

上午　下午　晚上

zài
再

"好，我不再打游戏了。我要运动，
运动，再运动！"伊森说。

Let's think

1 Recall the story. What did Ethan and Ivan do? Match them to the activities.

2 What is the best way to spend the holidays? Discuss with your friend and draw below.

New words

1 Learn the new words.

2 Listen to your teacher and point to the correct words above.

听听说说 Listen and say

①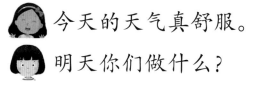

👧🏾 今天的天气真舒服。

👧 明天你们做什么？

③

👧 我没时间，我要学唱歌和跳舞。

👦 我要学中国功夫。

.

 我想在家上网打游戏。

我想去游泳，你们去吗？

我昨天看了电影，明天想再去看。我们的活动真多！

3 Complete the sentences.
Write the letters and say.

a 生病　c 运动
b 再　　d 功夫

1

我要运动，运动，再___！

2

我___了。

3

再见！我明年___来！

4

中国___真好玩。

⑬

Task

Paste a photo of your favourite star or fictional character below.
Give a brief introduction and do a role-play.

他叫 Michael Phelps。
他游泳很快。

游泳、游泳、再游泳。

她叫 Taylor Swift。
她唱歌很好。

唱歌、唱歌、再唱歌。

他叫 Monkey King。
他功夫很好。

我跳、跳、再跳。

他/她叫……
他/她……

Paste your photo here.

……

Game

Play with your friend. Choose a word,
do the action and ask your friend
to say the word.

唱歌	跳舞	生病	上网
头疼	游泳	功夫	运动

跳舞。

Chant

 Listen and say.

一二三，打功夫，
四五六，学游泳，
七八九，齐来做运动。

一二三，学唱歌，
四五六，来跳舞，
七八九，一起来活动。

放假了，时间多，
你运动，她歌舞，
时间用好身体好。

生活用语 Daily expressions

没时间了！
There is no time left!

我不太舒服。
I am not feeling very well.

写一写 Write

1 Trace and write the characters.

丶 丶 丷 口 叩 叩 吅 唱

唱 唱

唱	唱	唱	唱

丨 冂 日 日 旦 时 时
丶 冫 冂 门 问 问 间

时	间	时	间
时	间		

2 Trace 日 to complete the characters on the left. Then write and say.

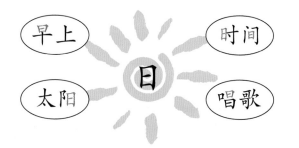

早上   时间

日

太阳   唱歌

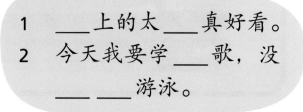

1 ___上的太___真好看。
2 今天我要学___歌，没
   ___ ___游泳。

3 Complete the passage to help the ant find its way home. Draw the correct route.

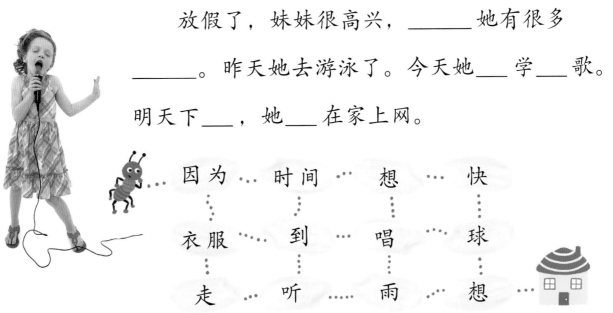

放假了，妹妹很高兴，＿＿＿＿她有很多

＿＿＿＿。昨天她去游泳了。今天她＿＿ 学＿＿ 歌。

明天下＿＿，她＿＿ 在家上网。

因为 … 时间 … 想 … 快

衣服 … 到 … 唱 … 球

走 … 听 … 雨 … 想

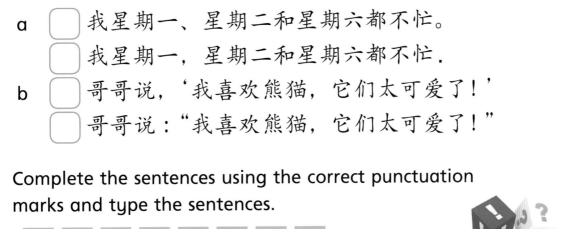

拼音输入法 Pinyin input

1 Tick the sentences with the correct punctuation marks and type them.

> Chinese punctuation marks are different from the English ones. Pay special attention to their shapes and usage when typing Chinese sentences.

a ☐ 我星期一、星期二和星期六都不忙。
☐ 我星期一，星期二和星期六都不忙.

b ☐ 哥哥说，'我喜欢熊猫，它们太可爱了！'
☐ 哥哥说："我喜欢熊猫，它们太可爱了！"

2 Complete the sentences using the correct punctuation marks and type the sentences.

、 ， 。 ？ ！ ： " "

姐姐说 ☐ ☐ 游泳真累 ☐ 弟弟 ☐ 你饿了吗 ☐

这里有饼干 ☐ 三明治和鸡蛋 ☐ 你想吃什么？ ☐

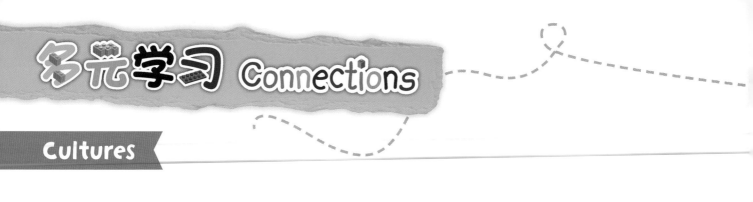

Cultures

1 Have you watched any kung fu films? Do you know any of the kung fu schools? Learn about Chinese kung fu.

Chinese kung fu (martial arts) is a system of fighting. It has a long history in China.

我踢、踢、再踢！

慢慢打，别太快。

我们跳、跳、再跳！

T'ai chi

There are various kung fu families, schools or sects across China.

Shaolin martial arts

我爱中国功夫。

Practising Chinese kung fu helps strengthen one's body and mind.

2 Can you do these kung fu stances? Practise with your friend.

1 Have you heard of Beijing Opera? Read about it and find out the secret behind the colour scheme of its facial make-up (lianpu).

Beijing Opera is a Chinese form of opera which combines speech, singing, mime, acrobatics and music. The performers paint their faces different colours to represent different characteristics.

| loyal, courageous | upright, unyielding | brave, reckless | fierce, ruthless | cunning |

2 Design your own make-up pattern for any person or character. Show it to your friend and talk about it.

这是我的朋友/
Monkey King/……

他/她会……

他/她的脸是……色的,
眼睛是……, 鼻子是……

1 Complete the conversation and role-play with your friend.

游戏

开始

Amy　Danny

1 下午有很多 _____ 。

2 我们上网玩游戏好吗？

3 太好了！开始吧。看，左边是我的照片，右边是你的 _____ 。

4 我们玩什么游戏？

5 我不想玩 _____ 游戏和 _____ 游戏。

6 我们再看看。我不太喜欢 _____ 游戏。

7 _____ 游戏怎么样？ _____ 歌

8 好！

2 Work with your friend. Colour the stars and the chillies.

Words	说	读	写
时间	☆	☆	☆
功夫	☆	☆	🌶
唱歌	☆	☆	🌶
跳舞	☆	☆	🌶
上网	☆	☆	🌶
运动	☆	☆	🌶
再	☆	☆	🌶
照片	☆	🌶	🌶
游泳	☆	🌶	🌶
舒服	☆	🌶	🌶

Words and sentences	说	读	写
游戏	☆	🌶	🌶
生病	☆	🌶	🌶
疼	☆	🌶	🌶
我要运动、运动、再运动。	☆	🌶	🌶

Talk about leisure activities	☆

3 What does your teacher say?

My teacher says ...

分享 Sharing

Words I remember

时间	shí jiān	time
功夫	gōng fu	kung fu
唱歌	chàng gē	to sing
跳舞	tiào wǔ	to dance
上网	shàng wǎng	to go online
运动	yùn dòng	to do sports
再	zài	again, once more
照片	zhào piàn	photo
游泳	yóu yǒng	to swim
舒服	shū fu	well
游戏	yóu xì	game
生病	shēng bìng	to get sick
疼	téng	to ache

Other words

放假	fàng jià	to have a holiday
够	gòu	enough
用	yòng	to use
还	hái	also
拍	pāi	to take (a photo)
叫	jiào	to ask
天天	tiān tiān	every day
应该	yīng gāi	ought to, should
要	yào	to be determined

OXFORD
UNIVERSITY PRESS

Oxford University Press is a department of the University of Oxford.
It furthers the University's objective of excellence in research, scholarship,
and education by publishing worldwide. Oxford is a registered trade mark of
Oxford University Press in the UK and in certain other countries

Published in Hong Kong by
Oxford University Press (China) Limited
39th Floor, One Kowloon, 1 Wang Yuen Street, Kowloon Bay,
Hong Kong

Illustrated by Anne Lee, Emily Chan, KY Chan and Wildman

Photographs for reproduction permitted by Dreamstime.com

China National Publications Import & Export (Group) Corporation is an authorized distributor of
Oxford Elementary Chinese.

Please contact content@cnpiec.com.cn or 86-10-65856782

ISBN: 978-0-19-082257-6

10 9 8 7 6 5 4 3 2